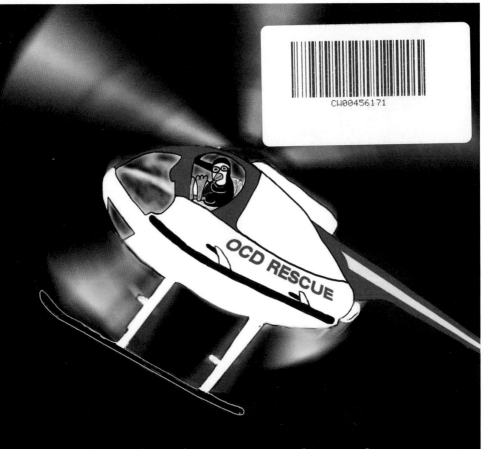

The little OCD book

One person's lifelong journey
with
Obsessive Compulsive Disorder

Hi.

This is a little book about Obsessive Compulsive Disorder, and my experiences with it over 40 years. This book offers no suggestions to assist you if you have OCD, as I am not qualified to do that. I just explain how I felt and what I did.

The bottom line is, I manage my OCD better after having seen informed medical doctors who referred me to skilled psychologists.

Most people know about the Compulsive side of the disorder, washing hands etc, and may dismiss it as curious or funny, but there is nothing funny about it when it gets chronic and the Obsessive side is not a thigh slapper either. Most people knew nothing about my OCD for decades. It's a short read, hope you like it.

My OCD started innocently enough, but it quickly gained power and turned nasty.

I was working on a car's steering mechanism in my father's mechanical repair business, when a thought just occurred to me. If I didn't tighten the nuts and bolts correctly, this steering could become erratic, the car might run off the road and the driver could be killed.

Worse, they could drive into oncoming traffic! Tens of people could be killed because of me. I checked the nut again, and once more for good measure. Anxiety started to rise, and I checked again, and again.

OCD has many forms.

If you are reading this, you may have OCD or someone you know may have it. It has many different forms. Knowledge of the variety reduced my anxiety a bit. I realised I was not alone. My cartoon characters here have some of those different forms of OCD.

My OCD started slow and steady, then became worse with rising anxiety levels. However, as I checked and rechecked I became caught in a pattern of rumination.

If you have OCD, you may feel trapped by different rituals that you must do, every time you do something. If you or someone you know has this, you can get help by contacting a health professional, like a doctor or psychologist.

This shark looks tired because his brain is overheating as he checks over and over to satisfy whatever he has decided was going to end all life on the planet if not completed correctly; and it would be HIS FAULT!

In those years when I sought no assistance I was often distraught, exhausted and fearful. Had I sought help with the right health professional, I could have saved myself lots and lots of pain.

I always thought my OCD was somehow trying to come up with a thought "so bad" I would no longer be able to function. There were many and varied attempts to produce that thought over the years. It was very nearly successful, but I managed to find the right psychologist, and she helped me regain a better quality of life.

There are many different examples of OCD, and the one below is another common one, although I only had it to a small degree.

Sometimes OCD crept up on me from seemingly innocent games, like not walking on cracks. This can prove to be problematic as it becomes a little bit more obsessive each time and anxiety levels invariably rise.

It might be fun to jump over cracks as a kid or just not walk on them as an adult.

Not a big deal until you won't let yourself walk on cracks under any circumstances!!

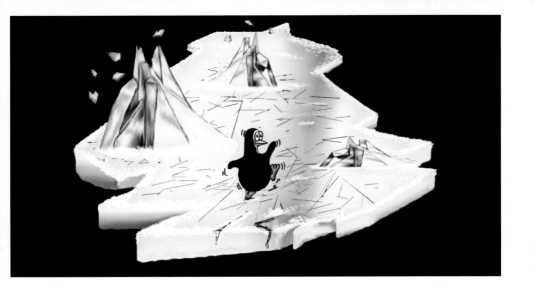

Suddenly one day, the cracks appeared everywhere! You are trapped and the game is no fun anymore. This problem can be cracks, washing your hands, locking the car, the list is endless.

If danger is present this can add to the rapid rise in anxiety, because you literally can't break away. Sometimes this is serious and you can be in real danger!

It was time to seek help!

My OCD rescuer was in the form of a psychologist - not in a helicopter though. She was in an office.

I had been to a few work-funded counsellors who hadn't pick up on the real issue, so I had to search for a while to find someone who was familiar with the treatment and management of OCD.

I was glad I was seeing a skilled OCD psychologist when I did. I was heading into severe depression at the time. Treatment allowed me to gain a lot more knowledge about OCD, rather than being at the mercy of something unknown.

Now I can recognise the potential traps and use the techniques that my psychologist taught me. This

helps to prevent me from being eaten by an OCD killer whale or something equally scary!

Why did I wait?

Why didn't I seek treatment earlier? The main reason was that one blow dealt by my OCD was such an awful image that it brought me to my knees, literally, and very nearly fried my brain. I was too afraid to talk about it, even with some psychologists, but enough about those good times, I'll get back to that shortly.

Logic, really?

Most people are aware of classic compulsive traits like washing hands, or putting everything in ordered lines, or checking the temperature of every piece of chicken you cook so you don't kill all your dinner guests. (Must remember to cancel attendance at Mary's dinner party!)

The thing I was doing during these episodes was checking that everything was correct. However, if I felt that the checking did not feel quite right, I had to do it again; and of course, it was never completely right, because I was living in an artificial, 100%-guaranteed world that does not exist.

For example.
One night at work, when I was alone, I had to turn off all the computers. Why did I need to do that? Well the thinking was if I didn't, the computers that remained on would overheat and catch fire. Buildings next door would catch alight, then the suburb, the whole country and finally the planet. Earth would soon be a smouldering rock spinning through space, and it would be my fault. Maybe the consequences were not that extreme, but I certainly thought a fire was possible and the building might burn down.

These are irrational thoughts, but I was not rational once anxiety levels started to rise.

Lights, camera, inaction.
When I was a kid holidaying at a house on the beach, turning any switch on or off was accompanied by an electric flash as the salt air had corroded the metal parts inside the switch. Frightening blue sparks flew whenever they made contact with the power grid. I associated switches with danger! They had to be taken seriously!!

Asking me to turn the lights out before I went to bed was torturous at times.

There you go, no problem!
Hang on that could have felt a
bit better, not quite right.
Try again. Great!
Just not perfectly right, might do
that again.
Excellent. That was good, maybe
just one more time.......

It's been an hour, I'm stuck here! You can't just walk away when OCD is bad. If you fail to do this right, people may die!!! I eventually learned techniques to help me walk away.

The thinking.

I think the main thing for me, the thing that feeds OCD, is that there is no black and white, there is no absolute on and off. Life is a high probability environment, but nothing is absolute, cut and dried, 100% certain. It took me a long time to come to that philosophical reality. So I lived a slightly tortured existence for many years, trying to take uncertainty out of life. Which brings me nicely to my scariest confrontation with Obsessive thoughts.

Being essentially educated in a mathematical and precise data accumulation field, i.e., mechanical engineering and surveying, I liked to know why things happened and how they could be explained.

Pure Terror.

Pure "O" OCD is about having unwanted, intrusive thoughts that you might harm loved ones.
I remember vaguely hearing about someone on the news suddenly going nuts and killing all their family. My OCD immediately kicked in, with its

quest to come up with something that I couldn't process. The thought pattern was something like this.

OCD: "That could be you!"

No, I would never do that!

OCD: "You can be never 100% sure!"

No way. I would never do that.

OCD: "Maybe, but no one can say absolutely that won't happen."

I won't do that; that is horrible to think about!

OCD: "Yeah, but you can't be 100% sure, can you?"

Just like to point out, I wasn't hearing voices, but trying to solve this OCD mind game was very scary and distressing.

Oh!

And so began a torturous few decades of philosophical mind games, trying to function in a 98% certain world, where I wanted 100%. A world where extreme anxiety about this had me wondering would I be committed for having such thoughts. 40 years later I learnt this is just another documented area of OCD. I wasn't that special, many people suffer this needless pain. It is just another area of OCD not often talked about.

Ta-da!

One day I was again battling the logic of these and other thoughts and I said to myself, out of desperation as I was totally exhausted, "That thought is not so bad, I can think of something way worse", and I did. Then I went on, "Even that is not the worst, imagine this!" Suddenly, I was making fun of these horrible intrusive thoughts!! The thoughts began to lose their power!! I had discovered that ridicule and humour were a highly effective psychological technique, and I had stumbled upon it. Relief was immense!

The thoughts still occur, but they are made fun of now, and they have lost a lot of their power to distress me. They are significantly more manageable now. I learned other techniques from my psychologist that work too, as a one-size technique does not fit all and OCD has a range of different forms.

I cannot convey how distressing the pure "O" OCD was, but I was on the edge. A knowledge of what Pure "O" was would have been really beneficial.

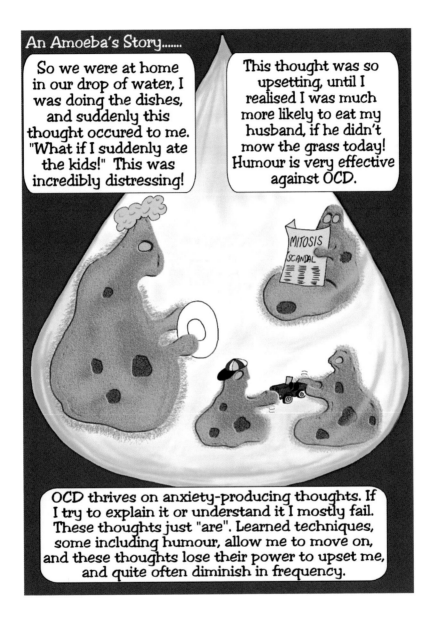

Still, I think I have won about $58 in the Lotto during that 40-year period, so it wasn't all bad!

A light lunch at the end of the tunnel?

So the bad times have greatly reduced. I have effective techniques that work for me.

In the last 40 years I have had some really bad OCD periods during which I gained a university degree, got married, had kids, and stayed in a job for over 30 years. Whilst there were very distressing periods, I count my blessings for having a loving wife, great kids and living a mostly wonderful life. Thoughts don't go away, but the impact on me is significantly less than what it used to be, and they have diminished in frequency. I can live successfully with it and enjoy most days.

Such is life.

I no longer analyse thoughts, they just "are". I manage them as they come. A lot of valuable experience has come from a lot of pain, but I wish I could have shortened that by finding the right psychologist a lot sooner. I wish I had known about Pure "O" OCD.

Other stuff.

One of the problems with mental health issues is that it may be invisible to the naked eye. People are a lot more comfortable dealing with physical injuries, things they can see, touch, and understand.

Invisible Anxiety

I stood at the train station many, many times, quietly gasping for breath as my chest was tightly clenched from anxiety. I looked fine to the casual observer, but I was seriously distressed. My psychologist taught me techniques to reduce that pain, by managing the anxiety. My wife said she felt similar pain watching me attempt to dance.

A word of caution.

One of the things I have learnt about OCD, is to be aware of people in positions of power who have a limited understanding of the condition. Amateur psychologists are everywhere and some can affect your career or your employment through incorrect assumptions and inappropriate solutions. You can become a problem that needs to be eliminated. Others do their best, and I have been lucky to meet those as well.

The best thing for me, was to find a skilled psychologist to guide me, as I participated in this journey.

The best person is not necessarily your stereotypical sombre, middle-aged man with unnerving x-ray eyes. I was usually in a distressed state when I sought help, but thankfully, I had enough reserves of self-esteem and self-belief to realise that not all psychologists were right for me.

I went to a range of different psychologist until I found one that I was confident in, and whose approach I respected and agreed with.

The psychologist who helped me is highly skilled. She assisted me in expanding my knowledge of OCD. This help was illuminating, and it made me realise I was one of many, many people in the same boat.

I find that I carry stresses
exactly how I carry dishes.
2 to 5 no problem!
Any more than that, and it
involves a lot of noise and sweeping up.

Some people are afraid to admit they have changed and now can't handle stress as well as they used to.

The mantra of "I work best under pressure" might impress at an interview, but I now prefer to know what my safe operating boundaries are. I am not trying to impress anyone these days, and from what I have observed, you may be trying to impress people who aren't really concerned with your health in any way, shape or form. Most machinery has safe operating speeds for reliability and constant performance. Good idea to find your own safe operating limits, in my opinion.

So where am I today with OCD.

My favourite motto is "Fall down seven, get up eight!"

I think this is a Japanese saying, possibly a Japanese ice skater. Not surprisingly, it has elements of OCD in it. Repetition for sure, but more importantly, "never give up."

I will always have OCD, it appears every day like the blue sky and clouds, and at times it will kick me hard unexpectedly. But I regain control quickly, a few annoying days or hours, use the techniques, then feeling better, away I go again. I have a fantastic life and am keen to tackle much more, so no complaints.
I have taken a long road to get to this point. It could have been so much shorter and less distressing. I cannot advise you what course of action may or may not work for you, but if you have read this, I hope you are able to draw better conclusions or have a better plan of action than I did. Knowledge acquired through a skilled health professional was the key for me.

I think behind my little frightened mouse above there is a lion. I have to be pushed hard for him to appear, but OCD managed that many times.

Thank you for reading.   Thank you, OCD.

P.S.   Don't forget to turn your computer off, tonight. (That's a joke! ☺)

Take care

Lex

Printed in Great Britain
by Amazon